Beauty & Forfeiture

ROBERT J. LEVY

FUTURECYCLE PRESS
www.futurecycle.org

Cover artwork, "Surreal Boat Sinking in Calm Water"; cover and interior book design by Diane Kistner; Adobe Garamond text and titling

Library of Congress Control Number: 2020947018

Published by FutureCycle Press
Athens, Georgia, USA

ISBN 978-1-952593-05-5

For Emily with boundless love, respect and gratitude
for your kindness, toughness and for being my guide
through uncharted terrain.
I can never thank you enough.

Contents

Drift

Thought is a beacon not a life raft—
and to confuse the two functions is tragic
                    —R. P. Blackmur

Setting out in my rickety canoe for the farther shore
of a notion I can only dimly glimpse through the ground fog

is about as good as it gets sometimes. You know what I mean:
how the purely conjectural is all we have to go on

when we give full sway to our true and rudderless selves,
how the cattail- and lily pad-choked swamp of our perceptions

is not just a limpid sump but a kind of destination, too.
Sometimes just floating aimlessly is enough to remind you

what makes it good to be human, and forget, for a moment,
that where you drift matters less than the sheer fact of being lost.

Should you capsize here, there is no life raft to save you. It's better
that way, to know always that the gloaming up ahead provides

no solace other than the mere fact of your continuance,
that the light toward which you guide yourself is never an answer

but a luminous and endless question that lures you forward
like a beacon into the true and pointless sweetness of you.

Belief

We still say *sunrise* and *sunset* despite, or perhaps because of,
the Ptolemaic model of our solar system long ago

having been overthrown by the Copernican. And we still
utter *O gods* galore at the worst and best moments of our lives,

at a loved one's demise or during a bone-crunching orgasm,
even though we've guessed that hoary, white-bearded giant in the clouds

may long ago have bid his last *adieu* to humanity.
Bottom line: Belief clings to us like white on rice. We'd shed our gods

if we could, likes snakes molting, abrading off that elder skin
of *thou shalts* and *thou shalt nots* like the dermal slough it is,

but can we ever fill the black hole that gapes beneath our feet
and ease the eternal dwindling sensation we feel each day

as though the story of our lives were about learning to fall
perpetually into the arms of some paternalistic

"other" smelling comfortably of tobacco, sweat and succor,
in his cheap billed cap and old, pilled knit sweater pulling us toward him

while always whispering *just the right thing,* how, though we are born
of starlight and uncertainty, we thrive in those sunless reaches

where the light of faith never touches. When I was young, Mother
told me *God is Love,* sitting on the edge of my bed at night

while I sweated in fear those ungodly hours until dawn,
and even then I didn't *believe* her, felt He was a punch line

to some existential joke that lost its laughs in translation.
What I did *believe* was how urgently she wanted to comfort me,

and how she kneaded her hands together nervously as though she held
some malleable and invisible dough. And it was love,

surely, that led her to lie to me about the eternal void
that hovered like a smothering blanket above my head, love

that led her to invoke a world that blossomed at my mere touch.
Mom invoked meaning even as Dad destroyed it with his fists,

pummeling me nightly with the knowledge that I was pointless
and obscure, bending over me with purple face and hands clenched

in futile rage against a universe quite unconcerned with him,
that left him beating my small body as though knocking on a door

for ingress into some other world that always locked him out.
And me? What did I believe? That the world whirled. That the sun

was merely a boiling mass of incandescent gas, which shed
its warmth indiscriminately on believers and unfaithful.

That there's an invisible world inside of things which, while mired
in dust, demands its witnessing, and lives among us like a ghost.

That what I believed had little to do with how the world was.
That the stars, the stars looked down on us with sightless eyes.

Wrong

Everybody's been wrong. Aristotle.
Lucretius. Tolstoy. You name it. They all
jabbed and prodded the universe's seams

for answers and came up with diddly-squat
half the time. As Michael Jordan once said,
"I missed half my shots," which suggests wrongness

is right in a way. I'm not thinking here
about those serendipitous mistakes
like penicillin, but for-real boo-boos,

like the time you told a young girl she was
the sun, which she took to mean corpulent,
and fled. Imagine we were never wrong:

Wouldn't our prized humanity suffer
something ineradicable, a loss
of stature somehow embedded within

our very inconsequence? Isn't it
wrong to be right all the time, to be sure
and sufficient as a stone, inhuman

at the very least, monstrous at worst?
No doubt, the preceding sentence is wrong—
too long, baroque, a bit too self-knowing

(a bit like this one)—but perhaps you sense
how hard it is trying to make itself
a body in this world. Truth is, we're wrong

just through existing, by being carbon-
based nodes of thought capable of dreaming
eternity, we've aggrieved the cosmos,

inserting ourselves into this fraught stew
of always-expiring stars and life forms
that ache, in our eyes, for a transcendence

that transmutes into gold. And, really,
what's wrong with that? If we are located
at the crux of meaning and non-meaning,

shouldn't we revel, in what time we have,
in whatever enlivens our brief days
in our skins? Shouldn't we, tumultuous

with loss, lose ourselves in this crazed hubbub
that calls itself a world? Isn't it wrong
not to—not to bite the succulent fruit

of every morning, let the juice trickle
like liquid amber down our throats, and take
a crazy, death-enraptured joy in what

propels us forward into every storm,
which is always the weather of our lives
and is, inevitably, right as rain?

The Swamp Road

Down dubious side roads, mere inklings of footpaths,
I have come this morning to a stagnant green pool
where aimlessness is its own end: the terminus

of the swamp road, a half-eroded track of red mud
snaking beyond itself through a sump of larkspur
and brown cattails thick as cigars. Quiet. So quiet,

in fact, I begin skipping stones across
the water's torpid surface, eager to dislodge
a frog or fisher from its summer doze. It's like that:

In the very midst of hoping to sidestep all
this rural muddle—at the heart of escaping
from the dogged humanness of each unblessed day—

you find yourself wanting to disturb the stillness
and obstinacy of a strictly inhuman beauty,
all that softly humming commerce upbraiding you

like a negative benediction, an insult
to the ceaseless, questing engine of your ego,
as, in the midst of seeking the forgivable,

serene pleasure of aloneness, you nonetheless
must, *must* insert yourself in the scene by tearing
lily pads up by their roots, causing stunned swallows

to cartwheel in sudden agitation. Why is
intrusion always our natural state of rest?
Why do we explode each stillness with a footfall,

take perverse and sweet delight in all that violence,
and why is there always some queer unearthly thrill
inside of us that seeks to center any hush

around our heartbeat? I think, perhaps, when alone,
when venturing far from any road, we are more
apart and solitary than any stone.

I think because we *think,* we are mired in constant,
rueful acknowledgement of always being central
to ourselves, a stunned awareness of a sadness

so replete with the unsprouted seeds of our undoing
it is a wonder we carry on into the night
with the heavy burden of grief at our apartness.

So I have come by the swamp road—not a road, really,
but a kind of slow journeying deep down inside
the destinationless self we portage in our hearts.

To be alone, I've come to see, is impossible:
Day lilies fringing the path trumpet the knowledge;
the frogs' constant chittering sounds the bass sorrow

of our irreparable sojourn in this weary,
too-taxing world. The journey into *alone*
is our sweetest illusion, a grasping again

at the notion we are central to creation
and so can choose to de-center ourselves willfully,
ignoring all the messy life trapped in the depths

of the swamp, forgetting it is a living thing
watching us warily even as we roil
its waters. The best hope, perhaps, we can muster

from within ourselves is that moment when we come
to realize we are never quite alone, never
separate from the churning, thinking zone that pummels

us with the constant knowledge of ourselves even
as we trudge endless miles to get away from it—
through muddled woodland, endless fields of Queen Anne's lace

until we come, at last, face to face with ourselves
all over again, waiting there at the path's end
with the usual picnic basket filled with ham,

biscuits, and a welcome bottle of Beaujolais,
thinking, *Why did we travel so far into dark,*
why did we sojourn so deep into otherness

as though we'd walked all day in a magic circle,
only to return to ourselves at the path's muzzy end,
and would we have wanted it any other way?

Zappa en Regalia

You can't write a chord ugly enough
to say what you want to say sometimes,
so you have to rely on a giraffe filled
with whipped cream.
                                    —Frank Zappa

At the edge of the stage in skin-tight bell-bottoms,
wife-beater and python boots, you were a slut
for the audience's delectation—

sweat sock bulging your crotch, droopy mustache
splayed ironically across your upper lip,
scrunched cigarette squished in your guitar nut—

loving how the crowd hated and adored you
as the stuffed giraffe spewed whipped cream from its ass
onto the privileged front-row groupies

throwing panties on the stage. (You slung them
on a clothesline strung between the drum kit
and marimba, then returned to playing

"Plastic People" at triple speed.) *Ugly*
was one word for it. So was *sick, depraved.*
And let's not forget *puerile, juvenile.*

In a country where you could do anything,
why did you choose this queer melange of camp
and crass to provoke your rapt audience

except for the joy of being pointlessly
obscene? And, of course, always *in control.*
That was ever the subtext of each note

you played at scarifying speed, a taunt
to the band, the crowd and to music
itself, which lay flailing, spent after you

delivered one of your trademark solos
eviscerating the aural spectrum,
replete with freakishly hard time signatures

that tested the limits of your musicians
whom you rehearsed mercilessly for days
until they achieved what you liked to call

accuracy. Touring six months a year,
interred deep in your basement studio
the other six, you had no time for love,

for family, for friends, replacing them,
instead, with blowjobs from crazed teenagers
and endless cigarettes. And the music, of course,

always the music. It flowed out of you
in a ceaseless stream of beauty, bad taste
and obstinacy, a middle finger

hoisted forever against conformity
(as well as militant nonconformity)
as you skewered hippies, Republicans

and televangelists. At your life's end,
bedridden, ravaged by prostate cancer,
you fought against the morphine drip just as

you had pontificated against drugs
all your life. Your three children, who barely
ever saw you, viewed this as a prime chance

to get to know you, but on your deathbed
you were staunchly mute, *paterfamilias*
to no one but the notes you'd committed

to paper over three decades. Sometimes,
listening to *Peaches en Regalia*
or *Watermelon in Easter Hay,*

their near-mathematical beauty, one can
forget the porn, smut, sexism and rage
that rendered your work fodder for critics,

and remember the demented genius who
worshipped at the shrines of Stravinsky and Varèse,
recall instead that whipped-cream-filled giraffe

watching you slowly vanish, with baleful eyes,
its improbable neck drooped mournfully,
spotlit forever at the edge of the stage.

Piano Starts Here

"Twenty-fingered" Tatum's arpeggios
poured like water off the keys in a wave

toward the unsuspecting crowd that sat
transfixed, soaking it in, dumbfounded,

as were Rubinstein and Rachmaninov
when they first heard him, as was Les Paul,

who gave up the piano for guitar
(Thank you, Art) after listening, knowing

at least one instrument had gone as far
as it ever could in teasing out

from ivory, wood and strings an aural world
in which "Body and Soul" could morph into

"Vesta la Giubba," or "Stars and Stripes"
appear in the middle of "Sweet Lorraine."

He burned his way through breakneck symphonies
without breaking a sweat, his note tally,

at evening's end, uncountable,
as he drew on the vocabularies

of stride, boogie and Mozart to create
music that acknowledged genre the way

tennis players accept the net as something
to master on the way to perfection.

That he was blind was quite irrelevant
as he brought sighted pianists to tears

with his technique, and they knew what he "saw"
was beyond jazz, past improvisation,

flirted with an aural landscape so charged
with surprise and awe each variation

was a birth, a coming into the world
of something naked, squalling, beautiful

and filled with life, so much so that Cocteau
called him "a crazed Chopin," so amazing

that a generation of pianists
has given up trying to play like him,

because he didn't *play*—he wrought, he forged,
a Hephaestus banging on his keyboard

until he made light even he could read by.

Urban Archaeology

After a class outing to Jamaica Bay with my daughter

Dead fish, syringes, mussel shells and crockery:
The news of the world draggles onto slate-gray marl,
rank detritus of nature and urbanity

roiled in algae-knotted stew. The children hoist
seines as, rubber-booted, they ply the muddy inlet,
wild for discovery, haul in a treasure trove

of condoms, crabs and brine-soaked porno
magazines, exultant at their catch and quietly aware
that it all, somehow, exemplifies the fraught lives

they inhabit. Across the bay the city's limned
in silver mist against a nacreous surround
that obscures and illumines their true origins

as offspring of a fallen world. For every shrimp
or starfish they find there are razor blades, crack vials
and bullet casings. No prude, the teacher explains

they are practicing "urban archaeology,"
while the parents aboard for the ride are
nonplussed at the environmental outing gone askew

with memos from a world they thought they'd left behind.
Today's Lesson: "Nature" is an artificial
construct, an un-Disney realm of robins, crackheads,

prostitutes, horseshoe crabs, all betrothing
fragments of themselves into a river that is fetid
with desire and loss, an unselective, piecemeal sump

of everything the city and the wild spews up
in profusion. At day's end my daughter's bounty
consists of pipefish, snails and the ceramic head

of an ancient doll, long eroded by the tide,
its lone shark-like eye staring accusingly
at the muzzy sky, a child's toy from long ago

cruelly tutored in the wreckage of the bay,
reduced to a fossil in a classroom display,
its torso swimming wildly to catch up.

Killing the Bat

A freakish flickering of airborne ash
slashes the night. Something feral has come.

Something borne of unlight and primal fear.
Something that reeks of everything not home.

My son immediately grabs a broom,
his first reaction to fluttering dark:

What is alien must be excluded
at all costs. (In the fireplace, the last spark

sputters, iconic, a sign of human
ascendance over all that is not right

with the occluding blackness that teases
his fearful eye.) The bat assaults his sight

with a wrongness so absolute he must
seek dominance, assert the light. His broom

could be a spear, his raw need so atavistic
he's reduced to savagery. In the room

something ancient is being played out,
something that transpired in caves and rude huts

back when *evil* was anything unknown
and anything unknown had to be shut

out from humankind. With one deft swing
at the chimney he clouts the soot creature

to the floor. He lifts it gingerly,
as though, in death, it had become something more

than canceled flesh, as though it were an emblem
of fear and the fragile paper fear becomes

under a steady human gaze. My son
has killed today, and what lies in his palm

is light as air and as improbable.
It is no longer chilling, but obscene

in its stillness, in its blank refusal
to be a trophy. He emits a moan

of something like pity as he carries
its frail body, almost incorporeal,

to the bathroom where he flushes it down
in a gesture oddly janitorial,

strangely malapropos. What he wanted,
I can tell, was something funereal,

something immense that might commemorate
the taking of a life, however small.

Now less victorious, he's a victim,
but so it is with dread of the unknown.

Dare I suggest to him it is himself
he inters with those tiny, splintered bones?

Raptor Center

At the raptor center the rescued birds
hunkered listlessly, waiting for a wing
or talon to heal so they could once more fling
themselves skyward with a screech, like the pure shards
of flight they were born to be. Visitors,
mollified by the fierceness they'd exude,
contributed coins, as though they had paid
for the privilege of facing their fears.
For show, the keepers let one red-tailed hawk roam
free, scoring hot curves into the chill air.
It didn't return the day we were there.
Jaded, perhaps, by its benign human home
it circled the meadow twice and sheered off,
without thanks, into kingdoms of pure if.

Snake

Under penalty of starlight I sought
you out in that Pennsylvania darkness,
groping in the August heat as crickets
chirred and cool jazz swelled from the farmhouse
down the road. Evening was indelible,
strung with fireflies parading through the trees,
each a small falling star. I wished upon
those living lights to spend my life with you,

but, coiled inside yourself, dark hulk
at the road's gray verge, you recited names
of constellations to this city boy
who, just then, was distant as Orion,
hunting strategies to snare you. How much
of love is deception? A soughing breeze
shuffled through corn shucks like cards in the field
behind us, a tarot of natural chance.

"Snake," I hissed—as though to hide from myself,
as well as from you, the fact there was no snake—
and you ran to me, terrified. The rest,
if not history, was at least one way
things might have gone. The snake was as real
as we desired it. The warm night held us
safely in the garden of our choosing,
and from the farmhouse no one called *Come in.*

Nourishment

Gray lamb gristle, flaccid chicken necks: Mom
always filched the worst and smallest portions
for dinner, made a show of it, in fact,
claiming, *I like a little bit of chew
in my food.* My sister and I choked down
sirloin or veal chops, watching her endure
rubbery beef liver, leathery chuck,
gnawing on leavings, offal, burned veggies,
whatever reminded us she was poor
and gave and gave and gave on our behalf
until it hurt. In that nightly theater
of denial it was impossible
to actually enjoy food; spring lamb
or lobster, rendered rancid on our tongues,
became a kind of anti-food, a sort of
transubstantiation from flesh to trash,
for it was Mom's body that we devoured,
the food that should have gone to nourish her
sticking in our collective craw. When we
drank our milk it was renunciation
in liquid form that we quaffed. Our hunger
was never satisfied, our sustenance
forever sauced with guilt, and the hollow
in our guts only served to remind us
of *us,* of all that waited to be filled.

The Weeping Woman

Imagine the afternoon as a rune
and evening the unraveling of a glyph
that thwarted you all day. Imagine

night as a partial elucidation
of the Big Questions you asked that morning
which tracked you, heavy-booted, into dark,

cozening your calm with unresolved
impasses that left you dim and speech-worn,
wanting more than anything to caress

the arm of the pale woman who draws away
repeatedly, who always has something
better to do than be comforted by you.

Your empty hand, left with a lingering
sensation of sleekness and soft, blonde down,
draws itself back, insurgent, indignant,

and the woman—plain and desirable
in T-shirt and jeans—is wholly absorbed
in her several anguishes, her lament

for the self she once was back in a time
when possibilities flickered in her breast
like fireflies. Imagine what it is like

to know with startling certainty you have
botched her dreams, left her beached within herself
like an empty conch shell buried in sand,

the good time you'd spent together
a sponge squeezed dry, simulacrum
of itself. Imagine you are not

just imagining this, that it's too real,
too flesh-enabled to be anything but
the mangled substance of your latter days,

that you've arrived at a place with no redress
for the ache that overwhelms you, as you
watch the sorrowing, pale woman recede

further and further away from you,
a dream of love forever sunsetting,
always famished, never culminating

in a soft, revivifying word. You
can imagine so much that defies
logic—and how beautiful to do so,

to fall endlessly forward into bliss
unmitigated by the certainty
that blunts and damages the enlivening

and bracing indecisions that lash
your days. Imagine, too, the pale woman
weeping out the length of her sadness,

the way she cups her downturned face as though
it were an immaculate fruit shedding
nectar into her upturned palms. There is

nothing so small it cannot be revived
by a perfect and unyielding phrase,
nothing so inanimate it cannot live

through a fitting word that finds a warm heart
beating there inside its hollow chest;
and, tonight, with you intermittently

sobbing over all that is lost, lovely
and irredeemable, I would tell you
to imagine, for a moment, that this

is how the world moves through us, a zephyr
chaotic and oblique, and all the words
only specks of sand tossed by a wind

that we can never hope to understand.
Imagine, at last, the tears engulfing
your hours are no more than a gentle rain

blithely indifferent to the human chord,
a mere effusion, a kind of dumb show
of emotions for which you have no language

but a sigh, and all the hopes you have hoped
are as pointless as the pain you feel,
meaningless as the kiss I would bestow

on your brow tonight as you drift to sleep
and dream of everything you've never had,
while all I want to do is stroke your arm.

Not Looking at Women

is so much harder than looking at them.
Easy enough to be like those local swells
on the corner—slicked hair, shined shoes, gawking
at lithe young girls, taut in summer dresses—

a leer on their lips, a deck of Luckies
rolled up in the sleeves of their muscle tees,
but harder to know when to avert eyes
from bosom and butt, to loft a fleet glance

a woman's way and, with a decent respect,
not to stare, give them back to themselves
in a swift gesture at once conceding
the painful beauty of their necks and arms

downed with fuzz, pearled with sweat, letting them know
they love each one in their passing so much
that they refrain from the stare, the ogle
that reduces them to flesh sweltering

in the city's unrelenting meltdown
of sun and heat. Looking and not looking:
They're not, in all cases, opposite sides
of the same well-thumbed coin, but currency

nonetheless, a transaction one cultivates
to give the splendor of women their due
without actually *doing* them
with one's eyes, without visually

stealing every delicate element
of their loveliness with a glance and grin,
by looking just long enough as they near
and then, at the right moment, breaking off

that following shot, so you do not own
their bodies but return to them a pride
they carry in every languorous step
across the street, in every hand sweep

of their long hair from before their bright eyes,
so that the act of witnessing becomes
instead a blessed acknowledgment
of a beauty too intense to capture

in something so trivial as a leer.
Do they want to be looked at? Little doubt
of that. But it is all in the looking
and for how long. It is all in the sense

of place and timing, the way one's eyes troll
that glorious expanse from head to foot,
and then, having drunk from the unending
fountain of their allure, becoming quenched

with that sweet, intoxicating vista,
and then turning away, not zeroing in
on that undulating rump retreating
down the street. Sometimes one can see too much

of a good thing, assault the world with sight
and leave a charred playing field of women
fleeing from the rapt eyes that follow them
longingly. Sometimes you need to avert

your glance from the beauty of women,
even if it hurts, and give back to them
their eyes, their hands, their breasts, their limbs, their lips,
restore all that intact loveliness to itself.

Supporting Cast

Wrapped in the cool, obliterating dark of the revival house,
hot light streaming dustily overhead, I watch the long list

of supporting actors unfurl onscreen, looking in vain
for names that might have surfaced years later with marquee billing.

It rarely happens: Never do Todd McBride or Irma Korver
appear at the start of the title sequence, suggesting

that the famous have always been famous and the obscure
forever consigned to play "man with cane" or "surly waitress,"

which is distressingly like real life. Try as hard as we will,
some of us, some of the time, remain wedged tight into the roles

we've been assigned, and act them to the hilt without a script
because the script has been burned into our flesh since birth.

Of course, a few of us may escape, rise to "second cowhand"
or "angry cop," but rarely reach the heights of "chief love interest"

or "charismatic loner." Is it just nature besting nurture,
the notion that we are all our own sad selves from the git-go,

that "third dancer from the left" is all that we can aspire to
if we're not anointed "leading" man or lady from the start?

What, after all, is a *supporting* actor but the steadfast one
whose shoulders the lead gets to stand on to launch themselves aloft,

propping up their painfully perfect beauty by staunchly
remaining less beautiful? True, it is so sad one could weep

at the unfairness of it, but we are wonderfully ourselves
and flawed and finally more lovable, perhaps, by single souls

than by the fickle mass. So to Tim Haft and Dara Jones:
I wish you the blessings of the innately inconsequential.

To Arthur Convey and Jean Benson, may you always fly
under the radar, and never, ever, veer to close to the sun.

May you all, when the final credits roll, and the lights come up
be buried deep in the audience's mind, barely perceived,

knowing that, in your obscurity, you were blessedly yourselves,
and, for a brief moment, made of the same light as the stars.

Garlic

is wafting from your pores tonight as you sleep,
a *déjà vu* of this evening's supper
of *pesto Genovese.*
                    I inhale its reek,
its pungent, loamy contradictions, recall
how the *ur* oyster-eater is always
granted pride of place for gastronomic
bravery—the decision to crack open
that calcified prison so as to slurp
the stunned, saline bivalve into one's gullet
seen as epicurean hubris.
                    But *I* give
kudos to the plucky soul who first peeled back
the purplish, papery skin of garlic,
plunged teeth-first into that lurid, reeking flesh
to discover its lusty ambiguities
(halitosis be damned), its malodorous,
dusky allure.
                    Tonight its peasant cologne
surrounds you like a second skin, and I breathe
the luxurious scent of the "stinking rose,"
inhale its thousands of years of history,
the way it's followed humankind like a dog
in heat, always lusting after us, trailing
us from barrio to palazzo, from
mud-daubed huts to five-star restaurants,
indispensable as sex or bread or oil,
a stench we cannot wash from our lineage,
a way of being.
                    Devoured by the bushel
in China, gorged upon by ancient Greek soldiers,
eulogized by Galen as a rustic cure-all,
it's been a palliative for everything
from impotence to the heat of the noonday sun,
from smallpox to stomach cancer.

There is
no ill for which it hasn't been adjudged a cure,
no misfortune for which it hasn't been deemed
the *primum mobile*— high cholesterol,
priapism, hypertension.
                                    Remedies
are efficacious in strict proportion
to their repulsiveness: Think cod liver oil
and all the little, bitter pills we're forced
to swallow over time; and consider, too,
the syringe's need to hurt, to penetrate,
in order to effect a cure.
                                    What doesn't
kill you, nourishes you, the old saying goes,
and garlic—more than its allium *confrères,*
the leek, the ramp, the shallot, scallion, chive—
calls us to the things of this world, reminds us
we're composed of shit and starlight, incarnate
nodes of carbon fetid with the whiff of loss
and loneliness, smelling of mortality
and mud.
                    Tonight you exude the humid stink
of *us,* the messy, mossy stench of our tense
compatibility, the "pong" (as Brits say)
of our separateness.
                              Tonight you are garlic
made flesh, a wondrous transubstantiation
enacted each day in the kitchen of life
where we refine our way to a blessedness
indifferent to sweeter fragrances, attentive
only to the sweaty murk of what's earthbound
and ethereal.
                    Tonight I inhale you
slowly, fall asleep with you inside my lungs,
taste the fetid, fusty sting of our common
heritage in soil and sorrow, the gorgeous
mutability (the reek, the stink, the musk) of garlic.

Desire in a Dry Season

In a forest wracked with drought
everything is extinguished,
even words, which might kindle flame.
Brittle twigs snap beneath
the prudent footfall of a mouse.
Leaves rustle like discarded paper.
A green forest sleeps within
the greater forest, like a bead
of sap entombed in pine
preparing to explode. There is
a ripeness squirreled away inside
the crevices of things where all,
all is hushed and poised for flight.
The woods are abuzz with sparks
whispering obscenities to tinder.

After the Storm

Independence Day, 1987, Gettysburg, Pa.

Only later, in the ensuing calm,
did we learn the extent of the damage.
Both of us had been through so many storms
together it seemed sad that the wreckage
was complete before I arrived. Huge oaks,
centuries old, were brusquely torn from
the ground by their roots. A bronze crucifix
at the seminary was a mangled limb
clinging to its steeple. The line of trees
leveled on the back campus left us amazed,
but you could see how it happened: The fine clays
that made up the soil solidified
over the decades and turned to sand;
all that remained was for a strong gust of wind

to wrest them from the earth. I think the storm
was less intent on destroying the hill
than revealing weaknesses—buckled beams,
root rot—things ready to give. From one wall
a 19th-century chimney blasted
the lawn below with a shower of brick,
the building's rust-red blood. How it lasted
all those years was a miracle: One look
could tell you it was waiting to collapse.
So if the storm was about anything
beyond itself, it was about release,
the freeing of things from their own failings
as though destruction were liberation.
I thought you'd see all this as omen,

but I was wrong, as with so many things.
You found escape from our common torment
in the world's bare bones unsheathed, that seething
landscape. You strode off across the pavement

into the crazed deadfall of downed branches,
beneath the shattered canopy of leaves
and lopped-off trunks, willing to take a chance
something else might fall. A stick for your stave,
you paraded around in the chaos,
enjoying it thoroughly, pretending
with your supporting mast at various
roles: old crone, javelin thrower, fencing
coach, Gandalf. It seemed right, this make-believe,
one more form of release, a way to save

some small part of us from damage. The sun
kicked in with a false dawn late in the day,
drenching the battlefields in a red-brown
haze. In that moment, there seemed no need to say
a word. We huddled in complete silence,
so unlike the rest of our lives. That night,
July Fourth, we recalled independence
the American way. We did it right,
celebrating with evanescent
flares of gunpowder our grand severance
from all who would keep us from the decent joy
of freedom. We wept. From the distance
came sounds of laughter. Over fountaining
sparklers we saw our years together fading

into something much less incandescent,
but livable. We slept. In the morning,
touring the catastrophe like sergeants
inspecting a battlefield's desolation,
we noticed how the very smallest trees—
young pines transplanted outdoors post-yuletide—
stood tall. Quite unruffled and perfectly
absurd, they seemed a quizzical aside,
engulfed up to their feathery branch tips
in debris. It appeared something so grand

as a storm could not find a way to slip
into their unassuming lives. They'd stand
despite all the wind's *sturm und drang.* Chainsaws
began frantically chewing up the dross

around noon as busloads of volunteers
arrived—an atmosphere of carnival
and funeral combined. The two of us
slowly became the *two* of us. Meanwhile,
we packed our bags, put our things in order
as graduate students raked the lawn
for broken glass, and ancient professors
propped up stakes in the vegetable garden.
We climbed into the car. Things were heading
toward recovery. Even the chimney,
which had seemed a lost cause, was being
salvaged: Driving from town we could see
workmen sorting through the bricks that had fallen,
gently, as though they were something worth saving.

Respect

Reading Neruda, I stumble across
the phrase, *the wasted honey of respect,*
which means little at first, though it's sticky

and sweet, and I find myself saying it
over and over, savoring it
on my tongue, its cloying viscosity,

the warm, thick syrup of its refusal
to yield easily to sense. Deference
paid out promiscuously is sugar

to the soul, I suppose, a shiny glaze
on the already-cloying sweetmeat
of acclaim. *Wasted?* I imagine such

largesse being all-too-often squandered
on flattery of the underserving,
bereft of nutrition, caloric

in contempt of genuine sentiment
and applause. I remember all the times
those to whom I paid the compliment

of my regard dispensed small coin
in return, reminding me how,
at best, we're all merely human, renown

only substantial as a shadow
that trails one like a sullen dog. Esteem's
engine must be stoked with the coal of awe

and admiration, but as time passes
the machine of adoration grinds down,
and we are left with ourselves, a fleshly void

devoid of regard. What can we do but
hope to venerate ourselves, lick
the last beads of honey from our own lips?

The Horror

Watching a bad horror movie last night
        was so good it almost hurt when the end
    proved too improbable, undercutting

the gleeful *Grand Guignol* that preceded—
        90 minutes of hacksaws and trephines
    as kinetic as a kaleidoscope,

and, finally, as repetitive. Blood
        will out, it's said, and out it came, almost comic
    in its stalwart capacity to shun

a scintilla of believability,
        which I didn't mind a bit. Only when
    the director tried to knit everything

into a neat ball that might roll over
        the implausibility of all
    that came before did I step outside

the splatterfest, laughing for a moment
        (possible without cruelty because
    no one who died was more than a puppet

jerked to and fro on the scriptwriter's strings,
        and all that shed blood was ultimately
    ironic and self-referential—less

life essence than liquid scenery). The jock,
        the virgin, the whore, the nerd—each in turn
    received their red comeuppance for the roles

they played in the story's machinations
        as the shoddy plot unwound with the sound
    of rusty gears meshing and unmeshing.

O it was a perverse pleasure to witness
        punishment meted out so discretely,
    a torrent of body parts and torments,

all designed to remind each character
        of the true horror of themselves, the parts
    they played inexorably in a world

reduced to the dual satisfactions
        of judgment and castigation rendered
    instantly. Perhaps that is the best thing

about the genre—its unequivocal
        simplicity, its easy acceptance
    of good and evil with no in-betweens,

no grays to muddle the deluge of red
        that poured ineluctably from every
    pore. Only at the end, when the movie

tried to put paid to the meaninglessness
        of everything that went before, when it
    brought together the virgin and the nerd,

resolved their essential disparity
        with the *deus ex machina* of "love,"
    did it cut the essential fuchsia thread

that bound the warped proceedings together
        in a way that was more comforting
    than scary, because everything that transpired

was so quaintly bland and expectable,
        so blatantly false and mechanical
    it made it possible to just relax

and tell one's self: *This is not real life, no,*
        nor death, these sharp edges will never touch
    or slice an iota of my own flesh,

and thus I can sleep in peace, without the fear
       that an insane-asylum escapee
   in a hockey mask will shatter my window

late some night and slaughter me where I lie.
       So I turn off the lights and tell myself
   it's all a sleazy dream of a fraught world

where everything that can go wrong will,
       where the house next door is always home to
   a family of serial killers,

that nothing, really, is as frightening
       as not having this alternate world
   in which to retreat, that what's truly scary

is finally pulling the covers up
       to one's chin, as though hiding your body
   from yourself beneath the sheets, the thick sound

of your heart ticking off every last minute
       in your ears until all you are left with
   is the inescapable thereness of you.

Vacationing in the Real World

The catalogs arrive, intimating
torpid bliss or sybaritic excess,
and we warily peruse their charms,
imagining beyond the close-cropped frames
of photographs, looking for key phrases
that clue the expectant vacationer
into the secret language of leisure.

As though flipping another dog-eared page
in life's brochure of possibilities,
I study you, your rapt concentration
on our desperate mutual pleasure hunt,
seeing you now as if for the first time,
an island on no map I know, no place
I have ever been. It saddens me

to think our long years of estivation
together might end this way—like a shell
washed ashore on some isolated spit,
bleached to dust and stripped of meat. Vacation
was what we'd hoped to be for each other—
accommodating flower-hung terrain,
gay cabanas of infinite comfort—

but to end here, in these dank backwaters
brimming with self-obsession, reclusion,
is to admit, not this union's defeat,
but how love can never be governed
by its origins. Mutability
is what vacations are about. Venues
shift. Sands shift. Coral reefs accrue cliffs

of circumstance. How, then, did we shipwreck
ourselves on this sluggish peninsula
whose oily waters deposit driftage,
with every wave-lap, at our feet. Have we
reached, irrevocably, our last resort?

The palm trees hang their heads in unison,
a natural bereavement. Something's died

within this jungle's depths. Something borrowed,
something blue. Part of me and part of you.
Oh, there are fleeting moments we bushwhack
to a semblance of civilization
and find ourselves on a pristine expanse
of perfect beach—clean, white as love's first touch.
Trapped in that dazzling net of sun-drenched air

we could believe it will last forever,
but it does not last forever. "Time flies,"
as they say, which, when I was young, conjured
images of clocks jettisoned from windows,
but now suggests some form of insect life:
Time flies, which light upon the rotting meat
of every precious moment, rendering

the evanescent *now* inedible
and foul. So vacations come to an end.
Our day-trips into each other begin
to seem perfunctory or forced. We're like
travelers who exclaim, "Ugh, more ruins!"
when confronted by the Parthenon. Isn't
tedium what the catalogs defeat,

each page a heaven tailor-made for tastes
ranging from Saturnalian ("Pirate Night
features free rum swizzles, a moonlight cruise
aboard the Jolly Roger Barge") to more
laid-back delights ("Bora Bora's boring—
sans discotheque—but for young lovers
a godsend at good price")? It's dizzying,

all these colorful pages, and the thought
I might not be with you some day. Maybe
it's time for not traveling anywhere,

for unfurling towels and chaises longue
in the living room and growing bronzed
beneath the track lights' warm, expansive glow.
The immutable as holiday? Why not?

We could do worse than bask among
predictabilities. So, my island companion,
we find ourselves marooned in this moment—
the blind eye of a hurricane
invisible to all except ourselves—
and I watch you, as though for the last time,
turn another page in the terrifying brochure.

Throwing Stones

Crouched by the swamp's edge fisting pebbles,
skimming flat black stones, lofting dun ovals,

I'm reminded of the admonitions
contra this pastime: how people living

in glass houses should refrain lest they wreck
their habitat, how those who are guiltless

(i.e., no one) should chuck the first nugget
at the fallen and depraved. *My* first rock

arced high over a stand of fat cattails
and landed on a lily pad before

skittering—*plunk!*—into the weed-choked pond
where it sank like a…you guessed it! You see

the problem: Stones have a burden to bear
in our language beyond their own grave weight,

freighted as they are with significance
of sundry kinds. Stones that lie still are deemed

delinquent while those that have been compelled
to somersault downhill are celebrated

for their staunch refusal to gather moss;
and getting "stoned," while no doubt pleasurable,

is a clear indictment of a rock's deep
desire to stay inert and dumb. I'm here

this morning throwing stones. Because I can.
Because this rough gravel, all these pebbles,

these compressed nubs of primordial grit,
let me hoist them like the little planets

they are, flinging them carelessly
over weed-choked water while I contemplate

exactly nothing. And I am a stone
as well, dark on the inside, unthinking,

for one brief moment at rest within
myself. I frisbee a shard of mica schist

across the vitreous surface of the pond,
not bothering to count its skips, concerned

only with the heft of it as I launch it
across the reflective skin of water

and how the water responds with ripples,
a kind of echo of my intrusion

into this silent world of sumac, weeds
and larkspur. Sometimes it feels as though I could

kneel here at peace forever throwing stones,
gradually reclaim the activity

from all those negative connotations,
make of it something replete, essential,

a pitching away of worry and care,
as though I were editing my own life,

deleting inessential nouns and verbs
that slowed my momentum in this anxious,

burdened world. Throwing stones is as human
as it gets sometimes, when all we aspire to—

over the gray and all-swallowing water—
is seeing just how far we can make things go.

Mayan Ruin with Iguana

Scaling the impossibly pitched last steps
of the pyramid, I breached a lip
of crumbling stone, and a foot-long lizard
sprang to life, skittering into a crevice,
reminding me of "The Lost World,"
a dinosaur flick in which iguanas
were tricked out with ludicrous dorsal fins
then photographed in slo-mo to create
and effect of enormity. (It looked,

instead, like terrarium close-up shots
amid a green riot of drooping fern.)
I recalled, too, Jarrell's curious poem,
"Thinking of the Lost World," in which each thing
sparks memories of everything else—
tapioca turns to peanut butter
to vanilla. Woozy at the apex,
I scanned the alien landscape. It was
eerily well-tended, mown almost neat

as a putting green by its groundskeepers.
I saw it promptly metamorphose into
a miniature golf course, randomly
dotted with edifices of a stark
and bloody race, as though mere obstacles
to best. *Putt through Temple of Warriors
for a nifty par 4!* Part of me saw
the lost resplendence; part of me could not
shake the sense I was on a movie set,

the skeptical part that, a week later,
flipped late-night cable TV in New York
to find the same pyramid I had climbed
used as a prop in *Beastmaster.* Each thing
recalls something else; everything's at once

unutterably alien, strangely
banal. On Chichen Itza's *Castillo*
I thought, not just about the Cretaceous,
but of the time in Queens when I clambered

atop the schoolyard fence, looked down, and froze,
stunned, sickened by my vertiginous self,
until a girl climbed up and talked me down.
Ladders, fences, pyramids: There are times
they simply mean *too high,* when the familiar
towers above us. I felt everywhere
and nowhere that day, in time, out of it,
and halfway between, while the lizard basked
in the snake god's stone maw, savoring air.

Wanting to Scream

Say you are hung over, noxious, fragile,
and your truculent, recalcitrant eye
finds itself magnetized to the minor,
inconsequential detritus of morning:
tarry remains of yesterday's coffee
still clumped at the bottom of the French press,
insolent sludge; adhesive egg-yolk glue
cementing the sink's crockery cascade;
and the dog, bright and yappy, cavorting
at your ankles, ignorant of the pain
that stabs stiletto-like through your skull down

into your heels. It's then you want to scream
at minutiae—rail at the background thrum
of machinery whirring everywhere,
the fridge compressor cycling on and off
with a heartbeat's dour regularity—
and damp down the whoosh of Broadway traffic,
(or pretend, at least, it's the ocean's drone
outside your window at 4 a.m.), but
you cannot finally turn away from
the ugliness of the daily. It dogs you
as you try to make amends for the night

before the night before, still evident
from broken glasses, half-eaten sandwiches
splayed on the coffee table, reminders
of pointless conversations about, say,
the state of modern music, that cadenced
with a clatter of dishes and tense, fraught
accusations (my *Coltrane* flung against
your *Dylan* like a Molotov cocktail
that merely sputtered against the baseboards)
that left us weeping/laughing at ourselves
for fools. It's on such mornings you would scream

for the sake of screaming. Being human
and fallible is so tender and sad
it hurts to merely acknowledge the world
isn't half what you'd hoped for years ago,
that the small, inconsequential details,
meaningless and vague, are what loom so large
in retrospect, that all the grand gestures
you believed would come to define your days
dwindle, and everything you had dreamed of
is no more than window dressing for dust
that accrues over your best intentions,

a gray patina discoloring desire
and lust. It's then you want to scream, but don't
because you never do, because the light
of morning illuminates the minuscule
indulgences of every endless day,
puts paid to the notion that the cosmos
is there to be plumbed by your intentions,
that your hope to unearth the large in the small
is nothing more than beating on a drum,
which is quite hollow, but booms nonetheless,
with a deep, empty thrum that sounds no note.

Extractions

Taken for granted, his teeth, when taken
from his mouth one crisp spring day, suddenly
seemed so useful and white (the clever way
they end-stopped the sad, pink sponge of his gums),
but when he removed his dentures at night,
his lip furled like a dried snail, and he saw
himself at sixty, seventy, eighty,
a generic skull hung with flesh wallpaper,
slurping porridge, remembering meat,
its tactile feel against each tooth. Later,
in bed, his thin wife snoring peacefully

nearby, the very thought of kissing her
seemed a grotesque violation, so he turned
away, slowly running his tongue
over absence, biting down hard on his past,
staring up listlessly at the ceiling,
recalling when he was whole. *Appendix,*
tonsils, teeth. Life's been a long extraction,
a fraught series of urgent removals,
as though what it means to be alive
is to donate all nonessentials
to the cause of entropy, the poignant

wearing away of all that was. *Marriage,*
children, career. These too, like body parts,
degrade, decline, depart in time. What's left
is the sculptor's detritus, marginally
a body about which shards lie scattered
like leaves around an autumn tree, a question
more than an answer, forever unfinished
and oblique. Even speech, once automatic,
blissful, is now excruciating labor,
each word enunciated precisely
like a desperate prayer. What's taken away

is more momentous than what remains,
sharp elisions limning the circumference
of one's days. *Toothless,* people say, meaning
"without chew," lacking facility to rip
and tear apart the raw meat of this world;
but, *sans* teeth, he imbibes the warm potage
of his latter days—by fork or spoon or straw—
and salvages for himself a piquancy
that swirls on his tongue, a kaleidoscope
of flavors with a savor of the past,
yet still with bite—*al dente,* to the tooth.

Shopping List

Yanking a Post-it from a faded pair
of jeans I haven't worn in years, I see

it is a crumpled shopping list, so old
it dates back to my first marriage: *duck breast,*

morels, asparagus, Sancerre. Who was
I trying to seduce with that dinner,

my then-wife? More likely, I was hoping
to romance the both of us back into

believing we had a mutual future.
One could trace the trajectory of desire

in the lists of delicacies we try
to *shtup* each other with when in love

or out of it. I remember the time
my first wife presented me with a meal

that reeked of unconcern: *baked potato
and a toasted English muffin, butter*

on the side. It was as close to *fuck you*
in food as anything could be.

Today I'm cooking fish soup for my wife,
a heady amalgam of Marsala,

cream, saffron and scallops, and the message
writ therein is ambiguous at best

because we are years past the innocence
of an investment in pricey seafood

yielding sexual returns, far beyond
those languid days when a few glasses

of Cabernet could soften the edges
of distrust, make either of us unfurl

like roses after a warm rain. Today
my shopping list is more banal—*skim milk,*

bananas, peanut butter, prunes—verging
on the geriatric. Try to make

a *fuck me* meal out of that.

The Flinch

Even now, when friend or stranger raises
a hand in greeting, my first reaction
is to draw back as though an electrode
had been placed against my vitals.
                                        It was
decades ago my father last struck me,
but the meat memory of those thrashings
lingers—a dormant convulsion
permanently embedded in the flesh,
as innate as the need to breathe or eat,
a defining part of me essential
as a heart, vestigial
as an appendix.
                        Why talk when you can punch?
Why reason, why implore, why instruct
when a knuckled fist pointedly hammered
against a face speaks volumes?
                                        Even now
I can conjure him looming over me,
hands raised, his flat, boyish visage obscene
with delight in the absolute power
he wielded over a runty eight-year-old
who only wanted to please, whose every glance
was a naïve questioning of himself:
What have I done to deserve this lavish
laying on of hands, these artful caresses
that paint me purple and leave me inert
on the living room floor?
                                        I was dining
once with a friend who signaled for the check
by raising her hand; in that fraught second
I lurched, tipped my chair, knocked my wineglass
to the floor. She stared at me, nonplussed.
                                        Time
collapsed in that instant, contracted around me,

and I lay again on the parquet floor
in the foyer while Father pummeled me.

Today what is it that makes me recall
a man haranguing his son on the street,
a child whose eyes I met, a glimmer there
of that encompassing fear that squelched me,
that still renders me parched, perplexed for love,
for someone, one day, to lift their hands up
to my face so unambiguously
I would welcome that caress?
                                    Convulsion.
Shudder. Lurch.
                    I flinch again at the thought
of those familiar yet alien hands
upon me, spasming at the mere touch
of flesh on flesh, as *my* hands go up
to protect my face, and I'm welcomed home.

Doze

Aslosh with meanings, our best words grow tired
of significance, stretch their arms out wide
like children yearning for a nap. It's then
somnambulance subsumes the old writer

who suddenly would rather estivate
like a snail, curl his flesh into its shell
and lie on the bed listening to Miles
or Mozart unfurling at low volume

from the radio. *Avoidance of work?*
It looks that way to the shrill worker bees
who dive-bomb the hydrangeas outside
his bedroom window. *A nap, just a nap,*

he muses, accepting that lax withdrawal
from travail, but it's another labor
to dive guiltless into this zero hour
and leave behind all the fertile language

languishing in limbo at the fuzzed rim
of his imaginings. His mind's at work
even now while his gray head is pillowed,
arms akimbo, one scrawny leg straddling

a hassock. The weary words gather round
him as at a deathbed watch, waiting
for some nascent inkling to rally them
to action. Sunk deep in the chill pool of sleep

the alphabet goes limp, quite exhausted
with the business of trying to make sense
of all this fragrant, squalid human stew,
and it would rather languish in nonsense

than do the hard work of trying to mean
anything at all. Nouns, verbs, adjectives
congeal, collide, creating a friction,
which even in the midst of his slack doze,

imply a warming trend, a surfacing
slowly back into the world's dry tinder,
and the writer shifts and stumbles upward
from the blue nothingness of his nap time,

slouches slowly toward the ancient oak desk,
where his laptop and foolscap lie like twigs,
waiting for someone to touch them, move them,
rub them together gently, make a small heat.

The Hubbub

Filigrees and furbelows on the flowered quilt
blossom into freakish faces under my gaze
as I lie scrunched up on the bed after a day
of work ("decompressing" as my wife likes to say),
but my mind keeps trolling, seining, reeling in sense
where none exists, limning grotesqueries, sirens
and gaggles of variegated trolls. Funny
how the eye labors to complete those blurred squiggles
under a fixed stare; same for the ear, which fashions
a logic out of half-heard words, how, yesterday,
a scruffy street vendor hawking "Tube socks!" sounded,
to me, as though he were bellowing, "Thoreau sucks!"
and all I could visualize was that hermit
hunkered down near Walden Pond, Spartan and apart,
selling simplicity to the masses. It's all
signal to noise, the pure ratio of meaning
to mess that keeps us both enlightened and confused.
It's like that party game where somebody whispers
to the next person in line until, at the end,
a garbled sentence emerges: *The frambled owl*
deliquesces at crepuscule. What's amazing
is that it's a sentence at all, that the hubbub
insists on resolving itself to something
tangible and real, even a pure fantasy
of significance. What we cannot know we labor
to complete, quite unaware that we ourselves
remain always unfinished, a work in progress,
a whisper in a dark room without doors.

Bird Feeder

Thistle music trills at decibels
too shrill for human ears though audible
to pugnacious jays for miles around.
Like buoyant chunks of fallen sky,
the fat blue boats of their bodies
moor amid millet seed, scattering
lesser finches and house wrens in their wake
as they declaim the avian hierarchy
with clamorous, scolding cries. All morning
on the veranda, I have been feasting
on these birds, nourishing my earthbound eyes
with the seeds of their beauty and violence.
As each arrives in turn to eat,
pirouette paranoically and depart,
I come to understand the breakneck pace
of their being, how they are flames
enrobed in feathers, ready to ignite.
They are perfect and horrible. What,
after all, is as stunningly
unimpeachable as a cardinal,
or as purely alien and hostile
as its vacant, waxy eye,
its manic brevity? Maybe instinct
is precisely this: *thought turned into*
action without a second thought. Minutes
fly. There are birds I can't identify
rustling in the rhododendrons. Something's
mewing in the pines. My guidebook
lies unopened at my side. Why should I
ask their names? They don't know mine. Possibly
I'm "he-who-sits-on-the-porch-and-watches,"
which is fine, for I feel no need to soar
except through their intensity. "Nature,"
I've been schooled, is what's outside of us,
but is it so? All day this sound of wings,
and the birds coursing through me like a stream.

When Stoplights from the Street Scrawled Skeletons

on my bedroom wall, blotting out the stars
Dad had glued there to comfort me at night,
I was torn between fear of the infinite
and the earthbound, between the way my mind
whooshed out towards galaxies and nebulae
and was hauled back down to earth with a thud
by those bare-boned simulacra slipping
eerily along the Venetian blinds.

Between death and the dark of outer space
I found little to choose: Those lithe phantoms
swarming the walls, elongated and fanged,
glared at me in blood-red or ichor-green
as the stoplights changed, reaching out to me
with tendrilled claws, but those luminous stars
also chilled me with their dying violet glow,
and as they faded when the lights switched off

I found myself soaring into a darkness
without end, which was almost as daunting
as my ruminations on the grave.
Infinity, I came to see, traveled
in both directions: outward to the stars
and inward toward that final, endless sleep.
I wallowed in a murky way station
between the two, playing a waiting game

that held me poised in a perpetual
dance in which being and non-being vied
for possession of my soul. I was young,
of course, and didn't realize most people
are content to ignore the nether poles
of existence, live doorknob-normal lives
where the portals at either end are never
opened, where the shadows that surround us

are held in check by the diurnal round
of work and love. It was so beautiful
to realize—at least for a while, in bed—
that I could go to sleep and wake again,
and the street lights would be gone, and the stars
lie listless, unilluminated, dull
on the ceiling, and I would slowly drift off
beneath the finite warmth of my covers

knowing that morning was a certainty
(perhaps the only one), and my waking hours
would be spent shuttling between the vastness
that hovered like a mist linking either end
of my days. Between icy outer space
and inner dark there was little to choose,
but I chose anyway, to continue,
while each night I slept the sleep of the dead.

Taxes and Poetry

Trapped at work, I trephine an article
about capital gains taxes, my fingers
sleepily percussive on the keyboard
as I suture a tale of upper-class woe
in hopes it won't bleed on the middle-class
readers for whom I toil. The gaping wounds
of my labors won't heal. I'm suddenly
stunned awake by the lurid poetry
of my life. I stare at the computer
terminal, its rapt complicity,
newly enamored of the mundane
and how beautifully it scans, the way
each line of my life is lyricized
by its disconnection from the sublime.

How long have I denied myself
the repellent poignancy
of pointless jobs well done? The meaningful
is everywhere, especially
within the meaningless. Just this morning
I considered an ampersand
for ten minutes: It left me much relieved,
a better man for this morass
in which we're mired. Truly, it is ourselves
we tax, with ambition and renown
beyond our least control, paying
out our lives in an endless coin
that leaves us richer only in
our self regard for every penny spent.

And when, towards midnight, the article
is perfectly researched, complete
and logically inviolable,
imbued with the requisite irony
that saves it from complete morbidity,

I can put it "to bed." Though not myself
as yet. Unpunctuated and unparsed,
sleep's closure eludes me, I owe so much
to wakefulness, to work, to unending
indecision. I read the text again,
re-enter the semantic maze, finding
my way back to its heart, the place where
my surgery began, poleaxed
by my own blood upon the floor.

Saturated Fate

Because a *fluke*'s both a "fish" and a "freak,"
finding the typo in the recipe
was like reeling in a lexical marlin

that so strained the line of my credulity
I felt at sea, the way you do sometimes
when happenstance seems too implausible

and you start to question anew your safe world.
Saturated fate: a simple error
almost anyone would lightly pass over

with a brief nod from the inner ironist
whose job it is to record such blunders
while not letting consciousness become obsessed,

but I was hooked. The typo would not let me go.
Nothing shook the sense of serendipity
that, in some way, this pun was meant for me,

a crux of sorts, forcing me to focus
on all I could not focus on, the way
I felt destiny-laden, fate-clotted,

larded with doom, and how this life, fashioned
thickly around me like a greatcoat,
was as arbitrary as the next card

in the deck. We're fat with fate, the typo
seemed to suggest. Our arteries
harden, clog with inevitability;

a waxy plaque narrows our vision down
to what's possible and what's not. Because
we're all kissed by kismet (that ugly whore

in harem pants), there is always the taste
of death—sticky, sickly sweet—on our lips,
and a mingled sense of satiation

and hunger that leaves us dazed, wanting more.
The typo swam alongside me all that day,
an invisible dolphin butting me,

half-drowning me, then buoying me up again,
like a sea cat toying with a panicked mouse,
as though I were a fish out of water,

flailing for purchase in the human sea,
and fate were a dark squall line on the horizon
beyond which we simply take our chances.

Evening Snowfall at Annapolis Harbor

...a man must live divided against himself:
only the selfishly insane can integrate
experience to the heart's content, and
only the emotionally sterile would not wish to.
                                        —J. V. Cunningham

Snow fell on the pier. Out in the harbor
pale clumps of flakes swept down to gray water,
a vertical harmony without wind,
and the world an articulate stillness
of muted, feathery mist, more beautiful
for its easy acceptance of change. I

viewed a scene which seemed in need of nothing I
could give. Dories rustled in the harbor.
A lone gull patrolled the pier. Strangely beautiful,
strangely unlike Christmas. Mirrored in the water
was no promise, simply a great, white stillness.
It seemed that everything was waiting for the wind.

I felt like some sea bird tacking in the wind,
encompassing all the world with my eye.
Was something needed to fulfill that stillness,
and was it me? In the passive harbor
I watched snow received by dock and water,
but only I was there to name it beautiful.

If no one saw this bay, would it be beautiful,
or is this white seascape, uninspired by wind,
merely a freak of snow and frozen water
in chance commingling with a thinking *I*,
the dark and glassy quiet of the harbor
reflecting back a far greater stillness

deep within the bay itself, a stillness
even in the world that mocks the beautiful?
The mounting evening overran the harbor,

gently spilling onto land, and a soughing wind
lightly strummed the rigging of the boats, which I
could barely make out now on the dark water.

A few ice patches groaned on the water
as the soft breeze coaxed echoes from the stillness,
a nonsense symphony of sounds that I
knew were not quite human nor precisely beautiful,
but something other. Listening to the wind
play a random music through the harbor

I dimly saw boats swaying on the water,
faintly sensed the harbor's deeper stillness
and how all beautiful things are, for us, like wind.

Chess with My Eight-Year-Old Son

Gap-toothed, Gap-attired, hunching vulture-like
above the fray, he eyes from his aerie
the carnage of our mottled battlefield,
strategizing my demise. Toppling Dad

is no mere *patzer*'s game: Grimly surveying
my spavined pawn skeleton, as though it
were the last impediment between himself
and adulthood, he settles down roundly

to thrashing me. *Winning's not everything,*
I imagine blurting out, unconvinced,
hollowly mouthing paternal nostrums
passed on like DNA from dad to dad.

My son loves me. He'd love to destroy me.
In truth, I'd love to let him, relinquish
the responsibility of adulthood
with one errant move of bishop or rook.

Losing would be succor compared to what's next:
I see him falter, his hand pause midway,
spiderish above the feast, deciding
which sweetmeat of mine to make his prey.

It's then his eyes go blank with indecision.
Work or play? I can see him debating,
on the cusp of victory or vanquishing.
He moves, an intemperance that snatches

a pawn but drains momentum from his game,
leaves his kingside raw, unready for a fork
with my knight that abducts his virgin queen.
His lady lost, my son begins to cry:

I didn't mean to make that move! You've got
To let me take it back! I'm determined
to teach him the hardest lesson of all,
how there are no real mulligans in life,

how the kiss you neglected to proffer
to the sweetest girl in your high school class
can still knife you unawares one spring night
when the mist off a field smells like her hair

thirty years ago in a gray homeroom,
how the ambition you never fostered,
the wager you never ventured, the poem
you never wrote are raw appendages,

that fester endlessly. I want to tell him
how the passion to conquer all of life
is double-edged, can nourish or negate,
how I once knew a man (very much like

his own father) who learned that futile hope
could be one's enemy, leave one's defenses
open to attack until you become
a sacrificed piece of your own history.

I want to explain "acceptable losses,"
how they're half the work of learning to live
in the same world as death, this place where
each breath threatens your most impassioned dreams.

My son stares down at the board's wreckage,
holding back his tears. Doing the only
thing I can, I resurrect his plundered queen,
remind him how we all make mistakes,

allow him to destroy me once again.

The Knife under the Pillow

The knife under the pillow was the plan:
to palm it one night after supper, then hide
the blade in my bedroom. I knew its loss
would go unnoticed. It was for my father—
a gift more pointed than the usual necktie
and cufflinks—the next time I was beaten.

I was a decent kid, so why the beatings?
One might as well ask if God had a plan
whereby unlikely sons and dads were yoked
together for eternity. I hid
the knife for weeks, nursing it for father.
Next time he walloped me it would be his loss.

Sometimes I stroked the blade, feeling the sharp loss
of the dad I never had, and my heart beat
a little faster for that *real* father,
one less rash, obscene. It wasn't in the plan.
So I clutched the knife each night, and I hid
myself as though I were a stranger with no ties

to him. A tenuous reality
suffused those days, and I was at a loss
how to proceed. Should I remain hidden
inside myself? Provoke him to a beating?
The knife had its needs. I itched to enact my plan,
but my hoped-for scenario just seemed farther

away. Time oozed by. I learned to shun Father
everywhere. It lent an odd unity
to life, this avoidance. Slowly, my plan
seemed less urgent. My hate and the knife lost
their keen edges. Even the weekly beatings
ceased, replaced by blissful silence. (Had

I only known neglect would have stopped the hidings
he dished out…) I haven't seen my father
in three decades. I never got to beat
him at his own game. So score it a tie,
though, as the years passed, I felt the loser,
knowing there never really was a knife or a plan.

I made it all up. Beaten down, my only plan
is now to hide the knife in safety, deep inside me.

It's not lost. But Father will never find it.

Kitchen

It is poured Formica or hewn fieldstone.
It sits in New York or the Yucatan,
Gascony or Fukien. It is rich
in modern utensils or one-pot poor.

It is where—on a star-wrought winter night,
their newborn miraculously abed—
a man and wife construct a meal, silent
in the separate provinces of knowledge

each brings to their solemn tasks. He, perhaps
adept at dicing olives, guides his knife
precisely, whittling fleshy purple cubes;
she deftly shunts paired, blunt blades back and forth,

cutting cold, sweet butter into flour.
Later, a *pissaladière* emerges smoking,
tawny, caramelized from the oven,
redolent of onions and dedication,

reminding the couple of each other,
their child, everything they've made together.
She sets the table with their best damask.
He lights beeswax candles. The child has not stirred.

No wonder the word recipe for *hearth*
is *heart* plus *earth*. No wonder it's the sound
of the planet's name and the sibilance
of breath combined. Our living spaces speak

volumes about us, but it is kitchens
that seem most nakedly gregarious,
trumpeting the pungent exigencies
of the race: to forage, slash and devour

and then to assemble familiarly
each evening to re-enact the story
of that unquenchable ravenousness
among one's family, among one's friends.

That same man and woman sit down roundly
to their meal, but mostly to each other,
in the fragile and bracing miracle
of savoring the same things together—

the bitter-sweet perfume of onion tart,
the fruit, acid sting of Pouilly-Fuissé—
as the kitchen warms them in its large hands
and the child cries out their common hunger.

Happily Ever After

Once upon a time, we like to begin,
perhaps because it satisfies a need
to both memorialize and distance
us from the legends we tell ourselves
to explain the dark unexplainables—
white unicorns in gardens, young virgins
birthing gods, swaddled babies in baskets—
so we invent a tense that's not quite past
but lives on in a place called *long ago,*
gauzy land of bounteous primrosed meadows,
endless promises. *Once upon a time,*
we soothe ourselves, because what other tale
would we tell? The one where the world's always
relentlessly fickle, cruel? The real one
where the wolf devours Red Riding Hood,

where Rapunzel, duly coiffed, remains
imprisoned in the tower? It's always
once upon a time because the boundless
ahistorical past, flowing behind us
like a remembered river on a spring day,
allows ongoing respite from evil
and despair, permits us to imagine
a past pregnant with potential recompense
from the snaggle-toothed and mustachioed
villains who would aim to invalidate
our every well-intentioned act. *Long ago,*
far away: It's a delicious venue,
because we can savor its remoteness,
slake our thirst with the ruby wine that hints
of blood and lust and our undying love

for everything that isn't *now.* It's not
that we can't handle evil's messiness,
but we prefer it packaged in spun silk
and furbelows of lace. Let's be honest:

Happily ever after is a goal
we recognize as a splendiferous lie,
and we just don't care. And, being human,
why should we? Wheels turn. Gears mesh. Death follows
inexorably. Why not allow ourselves
the luxury of an ascendancy
to a blessed existence unconfined
by anything other than our best selves?
Why not exist in *once upon a time*
where promises, first thwarted, are then kept,
by women in chiffon, by men decked out

in green velvet and a ridiculous
crimson sash? What's *make believe,* after all,
but the best part of ourselves as stories
we would like to tell but, in good conscience,
can't, because we know too well the tragic
consequences of hope, of longing for
the prince or princess who refines our dreams
to a decency ecstatic, sublime?
It's both the high eminence and dungeon
where we spend our days spinning out
those grand old yarns that weave us into what
we are: a daily summation of ourselves
unconnected to any past glory,
a moment in time, a mere node of carbon—
a person, a thing, a rock—unstoried.

The Perimeter

Central as only marginalia can be,
it splays itself at the ashen rim of reason
the way stars do, affording a chill circumference
to our grandest imaginings, a canopy
that both solaces and terrifies, clasping us
to whatever is inconsequential, beloved.

It's what hunkers down at the rim that moves us most:
omissions and elisions; charitable words
we forgot to announce decades past that might have
redrawn forever the path of someone loved;
the embrace neglected a lifetime ago
that could have salvaged the wreck of one's first marriage,

guiding you to provisional redemption.
Today, champing at the bit of mortality
at 3 a.m., eyeing the stars dawdling toward morning,
I am reminded of each tiny, engulfing moment
I let slip through my hands: of the lonely woman
who cried and fled when I told her she was lovely;

of simple ceremonies I could have rendered
to friends in need; how my faithless father might have,
with a gesture, recast my days into something
I could have possessed fully instead of this footrace
against myself. Marginalia define us:
dust motes that hover around our flesh, ferrying us,

like ghosts, into occluded night; and all of our most
sublime enthusiasms, stunned revelations,
consign us to be mere borders to our lives,
circumferences we traverse in disguise,
loci of indecipherability,
and when we seek to locate our dim, central selves,

isolate with a blunt finger's sweaty pressure
the nub of *us,* it's like trying to pinpoint
a tomato seed, which always escapes,
slips awry beneath a vain and prying thumb.
At last we are not there at all—or anywhere,
perhaps. We are like small beads of oil in a pool,

buoyed but scattered among a thousand random thoughts,
seedlings seeking root in an unforgiving soil
so hard-packed and recalcitrant it fights
our least importuning. What is central,
at last, remains peripheral. What holds us firm
against obliterating night is night itself,

a darkness at the rim of things so black
and obdurate we must submit ourselves
to a plaintive pointlessness that issues from us
like a furtive plant, which seeks the centrality
of the sun while collapsing earthward into shade
that utterly subsumes. It terrifies: the thought

of the fringe, the exterior, the gray husk of things,
that unquantifiable place we spend our days,
for the perimeter tells us all we will ever know,
so board each day the vessel of the flesh
with dread and awe, provisioned with enough love
for our sadly small yet monumental journey,

and let us go, together, in our little boat.

Acknowledgments

Able Muse: "Killing the Bat"
Alaska Quarterly Review: "Urban Archaeology"
Cape Rock: "Supporting Cast," "Throwing Stones"
Columbia: "Wanting to Scream," "Respect," "The Weeping Woman"
Harpur Palate: "The Horror"
Minnesota Review: "Wrong"
New Madrid: "Not Looking at Women," Nourishment"
Notre Dame Review: "Zappa en Regalia"
Passages North: "The Swamp Road"
River Styx: "Garlic"
Salamander: "Extractions"
Southampton Review: "Bird Feeder," "Mayan Ruin with Iguana"
Southwest Review: "Drift"
Sou'wester: "Piano Starts Here"
Tampa Review: "Belief"
Willow Springs: "Shopping List"

About FutureCycle Press

FutureCycle Press is dedicated to publishing lasting English-language poetry in both print-on-demand and Kindle (eBook) formats. Founded in 2007 by long-time independent editor/publishers and partners Diane Kistner and Robert S. King, the press incorporated as a nonprofit in 2012. A number of our editors are distinguished poets and writers in their own right, and we have been actively involved in the small press movement going back to the early seventies.

We award the FutureCycle Poetry Book Prize and honorarium annually for the best full-length volume of poetry we published that year. Introduced in 2013, proceeds from our Good Works projects are donated to charity. Our Selected Poems series highlights contemporary poets with a substantial body of work to their credit; with this series we strive to resurrect work that has had limited distribution and is now out of print.

We are dedicated to giving all of the authors we publish the care their work deserves, offering a catalog of the most diverse and distinguished work possible, and paying forward any earnings to fund more great books. All of our books are kept "alive" and available unless and until an author requests a title be taken out of print.

We've learned a few things about independent publishing over the years. We've also evolved a unique and resilient publishing model that allows us to focus mainly on vetting and preserving for posterity poetry collections of exceptional quality without becoming overwhelmed with bookkeeping and mailing, fundraising activities, or taxing editorial and production "bubbles." To find out more about what we are doing, come see us at www.futurecycle.org.

The FutureCycle Poetry Book Prize

All full-length volumes of poetry published by FutureCycle Press in a given calendar year are considered for the annual FutureCycle Poetry Book Prize. This allows us to consider each submission on its own merits, outside of the context of a traditional contest. Too, the judges see the finished book, which will have benefitted from the beautiful book design and strong editorial gloss we are famous for.

The book ranked the best in judging is announced as the prize-winner in the subsequent year. There is no fixed monetary award; instead, the winning poet receives an honorarium of 20% of the total net royalties from all poetry books and chapbooks the press sold online in the year the winning book was published. The winner is also accorded the honor of being on the panel of judges for the next year's competition; all judges receive copies of all contending books to keep for their personal library.

www.ingramcontent.com/pod-product-compliance
Lightning Source LLC
Chambersburg PA
CBHW070007100426
42741CB00012B/3143